The Art of Creation

Bianca Modi

Illustrated By
Amani Mohamed

Illustrated By Amani Mohamed.

Thank You.

INTRO

This book is my personal masterpiece. It was built upon the foundation of nothing but unfiltered emotion and feeling that intially, I had no intention of sharing. Somehow, these moments of vulnerability transformed into pages on pages of poetry. Somehow, pages on pages turned into the book you're reading.

That is the art of creation, at least to me.

It's the process of building something from nothing, the transformation of pain into power, and a near-blind faith that the setting sun will eventually lead to a better tomorrow.

I highly encourage you to read this book front to back, because beyond being a book of poetry, *The Art of Creation* is a story— a journey of transformation, heartbreak, and healing, told through observation and personal experience. This is second edition, which means it's slightly more honest, slightly more forgiving, and is the first introduction to some new work in the process.

I hope you enjoy reading it just as much as I enjoyed writing it.

With love,
Bianca

The Setting Sun.

One day, I was standing on the sidewalk.

I wasn't doing much else, until someone pointed out the half-setting sun. They commented on its orange pigment, and all the pinks it bathed in— it really did exude an unreal brightness. One glance, and I couldn't look away.

I had never seen a sun set this way.

Within the minute, my feet were moving, imitating the sound of my heart pounding. Both beats were catalyzed by a single thought: I had to have this.

I reached the nearest car parked on the street. It was baby blue and had no roof. Then I did something I never thought I would do— I pulled on the handle of this car that wasn't mine, the door swung wide open, and I hopped inside.

There happened to be keys— it was like God wanted this for me. So, I adjusted the mirrors, threw my bag aside, and put it in manual because this was my story, and I wanted full control on the speed.

I checked my blind spot and paused— a moment of hesitation. Then, I glanced back up at the sun's radiance. I wanted this. I wanted to want this. So, I put my sunglasses on, put my foot down, and started driving—

I don't get creative blocks.
It's actually the fear that weighs my hand down.

My garden grows abundantly.
That's because I tend to it methodically.

Soil patted by hand, water poured by glass,
I've fed it all I can—

You could say I have a green thumb.

I can sit there for hours, just pasting what I find onto paper; the apples, the trees, the upside-down flowers— it grows unaware of the laws of reality.

It's an abundant garden you see.

I just don't think it gets enough sunlight.
Maybe that's why I find so many weeds.

There's nothing wrong with weeds. The yellow pollen and the spikey leaves serve a purpose for many living things.

I'm just saying they no longer serve a purpose for me.

And sometimes, that sun-hungry garden will darken too quickly,
revealing truths and thoughts that I don't want to see—

I trip over them, I trip over everything, I can't differentiate my mind from reality—

that's when I'll put down the pen, step outside of my head,
at least until I can see things clearly.

I feel lonely, but it’s worse than lonely.
I think the feeling is more like:

I’m trapped alone inside my body.

Take a deep breath in.

Panic is what breathing sounds like. Give me 10.

Inhale
1:23:13 AM
1:23:14 AM
1:23:15 AM
1:23:16 AM
1:23:17 AM
1:23:18 AM
1:23:19 AM
1:23:20 AM
1:23:21 AM
Exhale

Panic feels like letting out a breath.

I'm sitting in my boat. I'm rowing, I'm trying, taking in all my breath, but I don't have to keep rowing if I can barely stay standing—

I can sit back.

I can let panic compress me, excuses, excuse me, I'm excused from counting my blessings— count your blessings, just stop thinking— with all this pressure, I can start sinking.

I've never been swimming.
Evolution starts screaming.

Screaming saying *I need to keep breathing,*
But *I deserve this* is what psychology tells me—

The water's rising,
I've never been swimming,

but if it meant escaping
i'd dive in head-first

i'll dive in head-first
deep thoughts shallow breaths

i'll take any exit
how do i escape myself

just let me let myself go
i'm tripping, tipping
over my boat

tipping and tripping
over and over

i'm underwater
inhale, i'm counting

inhale, never mind

finally

i'm sinking.

i am the waves, the ocean, the depth
i lied, i never tried to inhale
i simply let out all my breath.

come back come back come back to me

i think that's a hand reaching for me
i don't know i can't tell
the darkness of drowning is sitting on me

but i hear my name
they're calling me, a muffled voice,

just this once, try please

1:35:15 AM
1:35:16 AM
1:35:17 AM
1:35:18 AM
1:35:19 AM
1:35:20 AM
1:35:21 AM
1:35:22 AM
1:35:23 AM
1:35:24 AM

i see a hand, i don't think i can't reach,
i don't think i have the strength to do anything,

but somehow someway I feel my legs kicking,
my face lifting, my body won't let me let myself go,

almost like I am my own life support—

I break the surface. The hand grabs hold, pulls me out, they brought me lifeboat.

Swim or sink, swim or sink, swim or sink,
they wait for me to decide—

I take a deep breath in.

The Inside.

I cut myself open this one time. I wanted to see what was going on, on the inside. So, easily and effortlessly, a clean cut sliced through me, blood poured right out of me— so painful it was a painless feeling.

I sat back and observed myself carefully. I saw a liver, a lung, a kidney on either side of me, but those didn't answer anything.

What I really wanted to find was where the parts that hurt most were hiding. I even brought some tape to see if I could fix things. So, I sifted through everything I could see until I came across the things diagrams hadn't taught me.

That's when I found the core of my soul, and believe it or not, I found it was aching. Flickering out, losing more life by the second— I could've sworn it used to glow brighter than this.

What was I supposed to do with it? Tape wouldn't save this, even the glue wouldn't stick.

So, I stared at it for a second longer, took a breath in, let it out in surrender, got on my knees, clasped my hands
together—

then I closed my eyes and prayed for a miracle.

everything i write reads like dried out ink;
like i'm pulling words from the nothing that's within.

Sometimes my body gets stiff.

I rise and it sounds like a
lickety-split,

but the opposite,
more like a slow, tired,

rickety-sit.

Almost like the creak of a rusted car door,
or tired bones,

I think the weight of living has aged me faster than I'd hoped.

Nineteen, or ninety, I don't know anymore.

I know it feels like what ifs on my shoulders, anxiety between
my ribs, fear circling my hips— the weight of living is
compressing me, I think.

I think, I'm getting smaller.
I'm getting smaller, aren't I?

I need some measuring tape.

I was right.

I used to be 5 foot 6, now I'm only 2 foot 3.
I believe it's because I used to carry very different things—
courage and confidence are definitely height supplements.

When you misplace those, how do you prevent shrinkage?

Everyone's trying different types of medicine and age defying
mechanisms: melatonin, vitamins, serotonin, and inhibition help
you carry the weight better, don't they?

A weight like this can make 2 decades feel like 8, can't it?

I think I started carrying around that age, but now my bones are
telling me they want a break. They want cartwheels, backflips,
somersaults—

if I move too quickly, I might just break.

i've broken various pieces and parts.

a shower handle; water overflow,
a fridge door; milk on the floor,

i break many things; i am destructive,
maybe it's because i don't understand balance,

between love and hate, calm and chaotic,
one way or another, i tend to radicalize it,

and then i'll tip over, even further,
until eventually, sometimes, i fall o
v
e
r

and my heart will start screaming,
from the *just one more* i downed for fun,

then my neurons will join the party,
cause i'll give up sleep for anyone,

for anything, just to experiment,
like nails and steel are my blood and bones,

when i know quite well they're not.

and i've wondered why i do it,
and i think that i've concluded,

that it's partly for the *now or never,*
partly for the adrenaline rush,

and partly because i'm not nice to myself,
my wellbeing isn't worth as much.

so the self-treatment becomes toxic,
persistence becomes punishment,

but the ability to bend without breaking is validating, isn't it?

it is until you're bent so far backwards,
there's too much oxygen going upwards—

i get headaches.
maybe the oxygen gets stuck.

oxygen decomposes into carbon,
and that's what humans become when there's nothing left of
us—

there's a fine line between determination and destruction,

my body feels the difference,
i deconstruct myself in pieces,

tipping over, even further,
eventually, sometimes i fall over—

my world is just a reflection.

i think i have to rebuild myself,
before i can put the fridge and shower back together—

i built a bookshelf the other day
and it is completely unbroken.

Invest Just A Little More

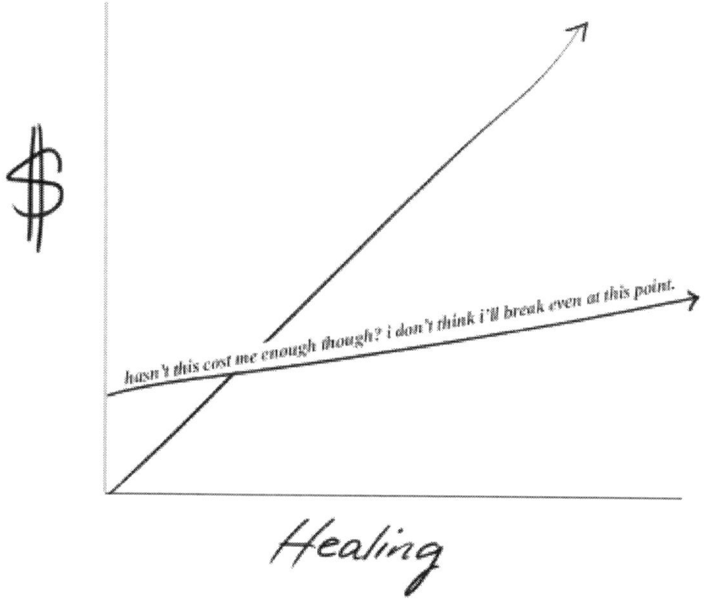

The Mind's Weapon.

my mind finds shiny things every day,
to use like weapons of obsession,

a thought twisted blade.

held right at my neck, it keeps me in check,
makes sure I'm not running too far or too fast,
makes sure I stay stuck in the mind's labyrinth—

like a fly to light it just can't resist,
forging weapons from my most treasured things.

compulsion creeps

like men, like death, like loneliness crawling all over me
i brush them off like ants
tiny legs tickling my feet to my neck

i brush them off, they creep back in
i can't find a way to exterminate them
but if i had a dollar
for every threat i obsessed over

i would be rich

and with that kind of money, i would never have to worry
because with that kind of money
i could buy a new mind entirely

and then the compulsion creeps would cease to exist.

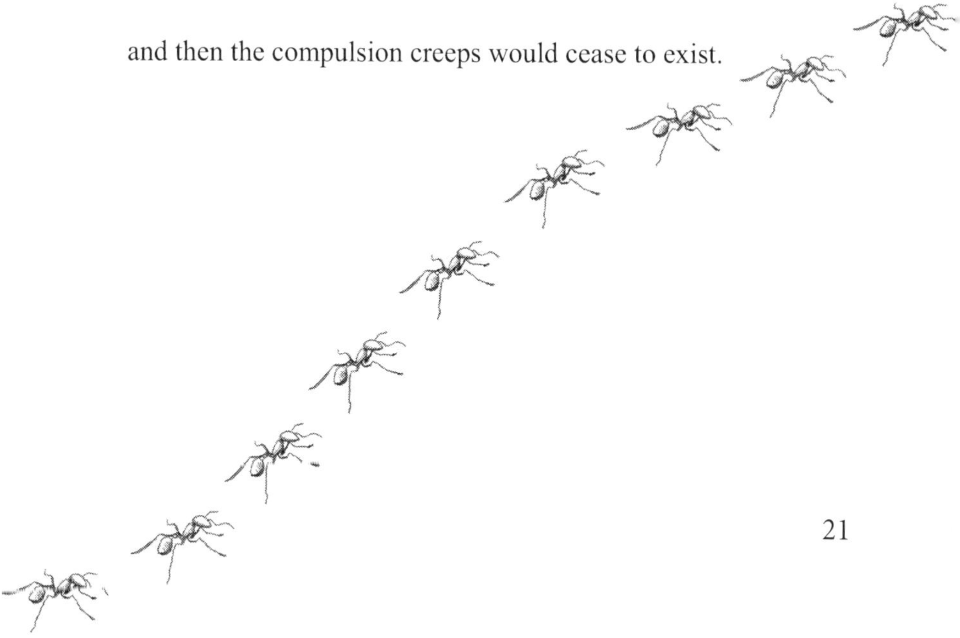

one two three four five
keep counting and eventually you'll find
that you feel ease at least one out of five
and you feel relief one fifth of the time

one two three four five
keep counting and eventually you'll find
that giving into repetition one through five
actually means going backwards in time

Let's turn back the clock.

I just don't understand how people become unstuck. I feel like time is a trap sometimes, because whenever it seems like I'm moving forward, it feels like I'm going backwards—

I'm 9 again.

And I'm terrified, because *what if what if what if,*
and I don't know how to get the *what ifs* to stop it—

wash my hands 3 times.

3 by 3 by 3 and I can't solve the rubix cube of obsession, because every time I follow through with the compulsion, I create relief for a second until a new *what if* pops up.

I'm so scared of what my mind is capable of because I'm 9 and I feel like my brain is threatening me every time the *what ifs* trap me with painful imagery.

Death, rape, injury— *what if* I accidentally hurt my family, *what if* my parents leave me, *what if* I go to the bathroom and get attacked by something. I don't know what's wrong with me. Someone needs to help me, but I don't know anyone who won't think I'm crazy—

at 9 years old every thought felt so real that I was afraid of everything. I was afraid of myself mostly.

Let me fast forward: I'm investing money and time into reshaping my mind by re-living these memories, and healing these parts of me, but I feel bruised and beat up after every session, so after all of it, I wonder if it's even worth it—

because I'm 9 +10 now, and I know logically, compulsions are just my way of coping, but on some days the fears still overwhelm me. I'm sitting here writing this because I feel like I'm reversing— different images, same energy: chest collapsing, anxiety attacking. I'm rotating between fight, flight, freeze, and the same obsessive strategies.

How do I stop the cyclical nature of doing things in patterns repeatedly?

At this point, I think I should medicate. I'm not mad about the concept, I'm just frustrated that I have to take anything at all; expend effort, work harder, think more creatively just to prevent myself from reversing entirely—

just to live life normally.

Now pause— I know I've been bashing on my mind for a minute, but I must admit that if there's a single thing the investments have taught me, it's that the fear, the intrusions, the compulsions aren't trying to hurt me.

My brain and its mechanisms are just trying to help me.

That doesn't make breaking the cycle any easier.
Time is cycling, but I don't think the hand started at me.

I think I may just be another person in a lineage of people who experienced similar feelings; those who didn't have the opportunity or the resources to heal the pain that's been encoded genetically— so every time I heal these parts of me, I guess I'm healing this pain's generational beginning.

In such context, I think backwards might not entirely be a bad thing.

It's been a year and I can feel myself getting better. I just need a way to not circle backwards, back around, stuck a decade earlier— I think I'm getting better.

Now, let's start that clock and keep going.

i will try again and again for as long as i live
because my greatest lesson is my greatest weapon

and you my friend taught me that
count again count again count again count again

don't stop until you perfect it
fight for your birthright to self-possession

and with that i will reverse the pain of repetition
reverse until i wield the power of this lesson

my greatest lesson is my greatest weapon
so thank you for teaching me my resilience.

Love and War.

It's interesting when your family's at war with each other,
mine have been at war for as long as I can remember.

Between battles of in-laws, identity, and immigration,
all that rests here is hurt and resentment.

So, with one side constantly at war with the other,
the two halves of me are constantly fighting each other.

It takes two blood lines to create new circulation, and both blood lines are upset at me for existing— my existence means that two brains, two parts so polarized, must coexist parallelly.

I'm stuck in neutral territory.

I can't pick a side, because I laugh with both sides, I can stand on both sides, and I see my genetic code mapped on the trunk of each family tree.

Look at me.

My cheekbones are sharp, but my eyes are soft,
empathy guides me, but I can raise my voice if I want.

There are so many divisions in my family, but there are no lines dividing them in me.

But then again, how can I not pick a side?

I've seen bullets fly by me and I don't know who aimed, I've seen both clutch their hearts, both bandage their pain— they're not both wrong, but both sides haven't always been right.

Let me tell you a story.

Once upon a time, there was a showdown. 2001. Bruised egos and beaten trust, I'm told someone left the house.

I just think honestly, if you want to win a war, you have to decide what winning means to you both.

Do you want an apology? Do you want them to understand you? Do you want to heal the damage created years ago?

Or do you not even know?

Maybe war is the only thing you do know,
the only ground you share, the only way you know to coexist.

My family is so full of wisdom, power, and intelligence, and neither is blind to these strengths in the other, but I think clarity is eclipsed by pain when they're together.

In me, they are always together.

I'm too alike one, or unalike the other, guilty ammunition is powerful, the war against me is resourceful.

Years of it has divided me into so many polarized pieces, a fight full of blame pointing, weapons and fingers, finger guns, it's all my fault—

If I didn't exist, would they have happily separated?

she was fed on the depths of fear, insecurity, under scrutiny,

i'm sorry excuse me thank you please
i'm sorry excuse me thank you please
i'm sorry excuse me thank you please

i'm sorry i'm sorry i'm sorry i'm sorry

i was fed on her apology for existing.

Generational Trauma.

generationally the trauma passes through us,
and our subconscious runs its hands through that knee-high,
knee-deep sand that has so many of us stuck in an hourglass—

i turn time upside down and my whole body goes with it.

sand in my mouth, sand in my eyes, coating my entire body,
i try dusting the grains off me.

i dust off my mama's belief that life is failing her,
my dad's feeling of almost there but never quite—

i dust off the fights that built me a sandbox to play in as a child.

sand stuck between my toes, under my nails,
so much sand that i could pack some up in a time machine,
pass it onto my kids, generational birth gift,

fresh off the blood line, here's the pain in your existence

but i won't.

instead, i turn the hourglass upside-down coating my entire body
in it, so i can play in it, acknowledge it, thank the sand for its
lessons,

and then with all my purpose and all my power,
go and pour that sand into the ocean.

A Sea of Serentiy.

i am more than the thoughts that pass through me, the ones that flow over me; even currents are present in a sea of serenity— that is exactly what i'm building.

so every morning i walk to the tap, with bloodshot eyes and shaky hands, i fill the bucket to its brim, breathe in for 4 and out for 7, push back my shoulders, and walk the same distance. of course some of it spills, and sometimes tears join it, but eventually i make it, into the ground i pour it, then i head back and start all over again.

because i am more than the thoughts that bathe in that sea, rushing like rough currents on anxious evenings. i didn't used to believe it. i used to get in and bathe with them.

i would let those thoughts toss me around, let them pull me under as i nearly drowned— but now i know different.

now i observe calm and quietly, as the current flows past me, as the thoughts rush through me, i simply let them be. i simply let me be.

because i am more than them, there is more to me,
there is more than this, there is more to me,

there is more than this,
there has to be.

I've been trying to decode the mind-made falling-off-cliffs and
break-in entries and I'm starting to think that my mind just
wants to make things.

A Letter.

Dear ,

I'm sorry I was so angry when all you wanted was the best for me.

You wanted me to have my creative imagery, all my stories, my worst fears, anything, anything to escape the reality we were living.

Making things was how you knew to be there for me, to tell me that you needed me, but I wasn't listening.

I just heard it as you versus me.

But now I'm listening, really listening, and we have a commonality: we both want what's best for me, and what's best for you too.

So now, this is what I am suggesting to you:
what if you and me, what if we made something out of our most favourite things?

The best kind of stories: beautifully written, hope invigorating, visions outside the ones we're living, like beach sides, book signings, waffles at sunrise, and self-compassion?

What if we mind-made the very best things?

Consider it.
— me

Catch 22: a situation in which both options seem mutually terrible.

Anger is uncontrollable. All she wants is to kick doors down, punch through walls— it's a blessing nothing ever falls apart, although it's no coincidence.

This is because anger is held back by guilt.

Guilt holds anger back like a friend who's trying to look out for you—

Catch 22

—guilt holds anger back like it's a punishment.

A grip that makes anger feel bad for her existence; guilt's grip is invalidating, suppressing, and humiliating— of course, this makes anger even more angry.

So eventually, she drips out silently until she no longer wants to kick that door down, she wants to unhinge it piece by piece, slowly and methodically.

I would argue that kind of rage is the most terrifying.

Now, with anger moved over, guilt has room to take over— guilt is a homebody.

She makes a home inside of me, eats all my food, inflates electricity. I've asked her to leave nicely, tried eviction forcefully, but somehow, someway, I always end up feeling guilty.

So, what can I do? Except move aside as anger and guilt go to war; I guess I'm just a carcass for my emotions to control—

these are my options, so tell me, which is less worse?

Bianca Modi

This Walk Called My Life.

as i retrace my steps down the walk called my life,
i'm noticing how words have cut me like knives.

honestly, i didn't even realize, until i saw my wounds looked less like blood, and more like words that spelled worthless—

selfish, careless, and useless
at first, i couldn't believe it.

because in my world, words have always been a source of wisdom, the choice of worship, my type of winning, and my form of wellness.

so i couldn't believe that my greatest weapon could also be my greatest weakness. although, it makes sense if you think about it.

my mind values words like water, so of course, something with that much power has the power to both wealth and wither—

rain grows and floods can kill us

so perhaps if i hadn't missed this pain initially, i would've wrapped my wounds adequately, used the right remedies, known exactly what parts needed treating—

although perhaps, it's not that i missed this pain initially.
perhaps i simply underestimated the power of words entirely,

because i used to say words are just words,
write them down and they're gone,

right?
wrong.

the written word waits and waits and waits, until the weight of
word becomes thought, and thought becomes belief—

write out exactly who you want to be

so, if you allow the worst words in, they might just damage your
self-esteem, cut and bleed your skin self-faith deep—

so now as i retrace my steps down the walk called my life,
i'm noticing a path i don't recognize,

one on which i will wash my wounds and weave my worth—

one word at a time,
i'm building the sky.

in vowels, in alphabet, using pronouns to announce my presence, exactly who i've always been,

in my first language, mother tongue, i'm writing out the stars and sun— they look just like me, glow just like me, i am more than enough for this sky i'm building,

so really, i'm building myself out of nothing, one word at a time, i'm building the sky, from nothing and no one but these words that rest inside me.

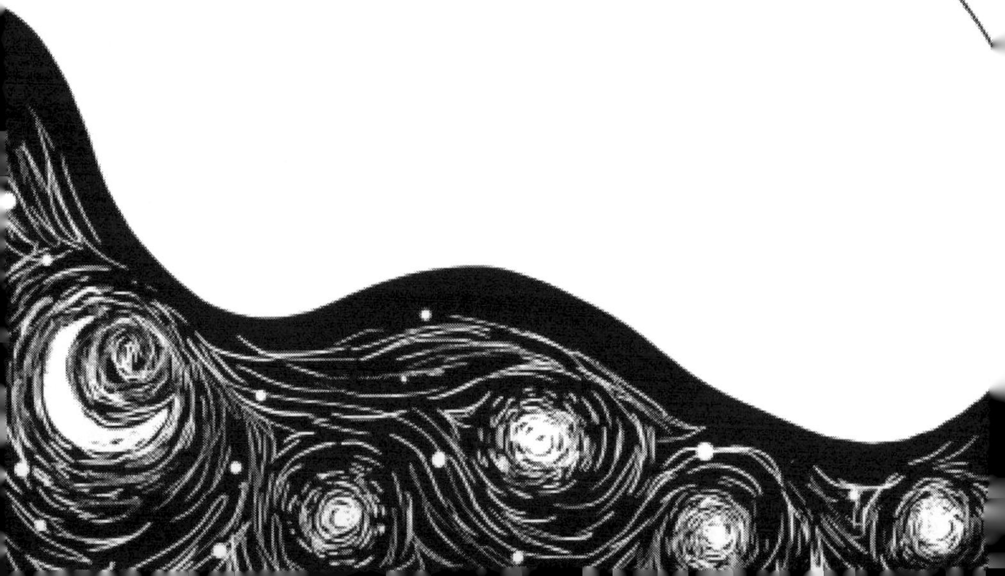

The Horses.

Whimsicality is my speciality,
wouldn't you agree?

My verses lineup like horses,
passionate but ordinary,

Count one, count two, count three,
they all stand in perfect formation,

Feed a horse grass: it'll laugh, pat its back: it'll dance,
but the horse will still want to be free,

Really, it's the master dancing to its own beat,
with all these beats the horse will be afraid to leave,

My whimsicality is synonymous for worried,
if I had it my way, I wouldn't line them up,

I'd spit verses onto corners of pages, on keyboards, on the
floor, I'd disarrange them until you couldn't count one, count
two, count three—

My verses would run free if my subconscious wasn't the master
of my conscious poetry.

Beating me up with sticks of fear and doubt,
the creator creates things that have never been done.

But that's only if you let the horses run.

let the mind run free.

I'm tired of being told what to do.

My mind and my heart speak in rhymes, in requirements; I love them but sometimes I just need them to be quiet—

I'm over it.
Let me walk you through it.

My to do list:

- ~~wake up~~
- ~~brush teeth~~
- ~~listen to the broken records~~
    - ~~in this order: you're useless, be afraid, don't be stupid, take more risks, think logically, what makes you think you deserve happiness—~~
    - today, we're not doing this.

Today I'm not waking from dread,
today I'm rising up from bed.

Forget brushing my teeth, let's go straight to dessert. I'm hungry so I'm eating, I'm angry so I'm yelling, I'm excited so I'm singing, I'm happy so I'm dancing—

wait, while we're here, let's go cliff jumping, skydiving, I'm afraid of heights but I'm just gonna stop scaring myself. rules are meant to be broken and my brain has made so many

enough is enough is enough is enough even periods and punctuation can't stop me i'm going all in, this was going to be a piece full of thematic symbolism and literary talent but who cares my words are priceless because

why? because they're **mine**

see what I did there? pretty cool right? I literally have no limits, and that is my weapon. I wonder what other amazing things I can create once I let myself create without fear, without limit, without a to-do list—

without telling myself what to do.

The Yellow Path.

take care of yourself hun, because one day,
one day as i was walking down a yellow path,
under dying trees, past empty playgrounds,
my breath was heavy, my soles were aching,
it started to rain.

it started to rain, so i took out my yellow umbrella,
i'm so thankful i packed my yellow umbrella that day,
but you know what really happened,
i took out that yellow umbrella, stared at it for 3,
then i put that yellow umbrella away.

i stopped in my tracks, and stopped in my head,
i stopped, and listened to the rain instead,
it said a few words, so quick yet so calm,
it said something along the lines of,
listen, your bones want to dance with us.

so, i took off my shoes, and i took off my socks,
i took off my jacket, and i took off my doubt,
then i saw a family of yellow ducks cross,
they seemed to be doing a one two step.

i took a one two step and followed them,
i walked straight into puddles, then i did it again,
this time i splashed in them, danced in them,
i felt my sole ache fade.

a few steps later some yellow boots stepped in my way,
they reminded me of the ones i had given up,
for the yellow path that greyed me out,
so i closed my eyes, kneeled to the ground,
took a breath in and put yellow on.

i stood, realizing everything i'd given up,
for a yellow path i didn't really want,
so i exhaled all that heavy breath in my lungs,
cupped my hands up to the sky, water filled them,

and i stood in the rain drenched in freedom.

The only paradise you can truly have is within you.

It seemed like the closer I got, the farther the sun did.

Blood flooded my mouth, and stress flooded my chest— I wanted this setting sun so bad. I couldn't lose it. I couldn't miss this. I started pushing my limits.

I pushed 20 over the limit, and then 30. Signs telling me to slow down flew right past me. I saw the danger, I knew this was unhealthy, but I think in this case the sun's light was blinding.

20, 30, 40,

I passed buildings that used to inspire, and trees I used to admire, like the things that used to be my focus were now no more than peripheral vision to me.

40, 30, 20

I slowed at a red light. I clenched my teeth, frustrated. The light stayed still forever so I reached for my bag. I paused, realizing it felt lighter.

Half glancing at the road, I leaned over to unzip it, and reached inside. I reached further, realizing what was missing. I checked the smaller pocket, frantic now. Seconds later, I exhaled in defeat, realizing what I had forgotten.

I had left my confidence and trust on the sidewalk. Biting down the regret I felt at losing my possessions, I glanced at the rear view, thinking I could go back for them.

But then I noticed that the sky had begun to take on a blue, starry light. I threw the bag into the back. Desire to reach the sunset had transformed into desperation. I was desperate to prove myself.

I drove faster.
I watched as it dipped further.

I floored the accelerator.

I watched as the sun disappeared.

I slowed to a stop. I choked out a cough, and the cough turned into a sob. A sob turned into the shaking of my entire body, so heavy and so intense that I needed to throw up. But nothing would come up.

I almost had it. It was practically handed to me. What did I do wrong? It was all my fault, it was always my fault, and with those words bouncing off the walls of my brain, my sobs died out into silence.

I don't really have a muse,
but I think love has a way of drawing the words out of you.

Heartbreak is my favourite muse.

It's a master at the transfer of words from my tears to my tongue, creating a paper that is so intricately pen-filled— it astounds me.

Though, it takes more than a *somebody* to extract that kind of poetry. It takes self-investment.

Almost like investing every part of me, time, secrets, trust, energy. I lay down all my cards in offering, heart open, everything's bleeding—

I take the gamble that my all is worth something.

Because when I lose a bet, my mind blames me, turns me against me— *what's wrong with you, what's wrong with me*— until in between all that anger and pain, the truth I no longer want my own company.

That kind of heartbreak aches differently.

It's an ache that expands from my chest to my limbs, waking up disappointed that I'm stuck in the brain I have, the package I'm in—

It holds a strange familiarity.

Almost like it's always been in me, a younger version of me, one who felt at fault, guilty.

Maybe that's why it feels oddly comforting.
Maybe that's why I can't stop gambling.

So, if heart break's my muse, maybe my muse is just me.
I create my own inspiration and create my own suffering.

Now my eyes are burning, my tongue is drying, my fingers are aching, and my pen is empty,

but this is the page, so do you see what I mean?

people in my sensory surroundings are drinking,
or maybe are drunk on

Love,
Lust,
Pain,
and Alcohol.

but let's be honest, if you asked me which,
i couldn't tell you the difference,

here's the difference:

the second is terrifying, the third is comforting,
the first one is hell, and the fourth destroys clarity,

because one night this girl fell right into island country.

into blue oceans, she met a mermaid, drunk on love,
until she realized it had been the lochness monster himself.

it took a(a) meeting to see that one.
have you ever seen one?

fiery scales and radiant warmth,
now you're in their arms, and all burned out—

she shared her story with clairvoyance:
the line between heaven and hell is subjective.

walk it, fall, you're addicted now,
falling for brown oceans, or in dirty bathroom stalls.

are you falling for him, for her, for them?
or did you just trip on one-two many toxins?

maybe it's the second type of chemical addiction.
skin on skin is dopamine invigorating,
and pills on tongue can metabolize the ache of living—

but just for fun, right?
it's all just for fun, right?

or is fun just a synonym for filling lackluster selflove,
quadrable whammy—

Love,
Lust,
Pain,
And Alcohol.

the first is the hell because it can shapeshift into any of the above.

maybe that's why i sip carefully, and think you should tread cautiously— the girl ended her story with a soft request,

don't pour your drinks if you can't live without them.

i want you

i want you
but really i want you to

put that bottle down, man spit it out
i can't help you with broken glass in your mouth

wash your tongue, and watch your mouth
because i refuse to cut myself

harsh, but i'm telling it as it is
what i'm trying to tell you is

you're not yourself un-sober
so un-lock that pain from your liver

and pour it out clear into purpose
onto paper, poetic genius, really any treatment

i know the pain you've had to cope with
but you deserve so much more than this

so when you're ready, i'm here for it
i'll cup my hands, and wipe your lips

clean the cuts, and clean the glass
when you decide to take care of yourself.

I feel so much empathy, it embraces me,
like your arms around me, it holds me—

I'm so sorry.

I said what I said with a throat choking on anxiety,
self-doubt, obsession, that year was a mess for me.

But I won't make excuses,
I said what I said.

And I'm sorry.

I feel so much empathy, it eats at me,
like a guilty monster that creeps and crawls over me.

I feed him with apologies.

Crying in *could've done it differently*, replaying it repeatedly,
and every single night that monster sleeps next to me—

"are you sure the monster's really me?"

It's been 11 months and I don't know what to believe.
I just know he's eating away the best parts of me.

So, I wish you the very best, and I hope you're happy, but I just
can't keep feeding this feeling—

It's time for me to set the monster free.

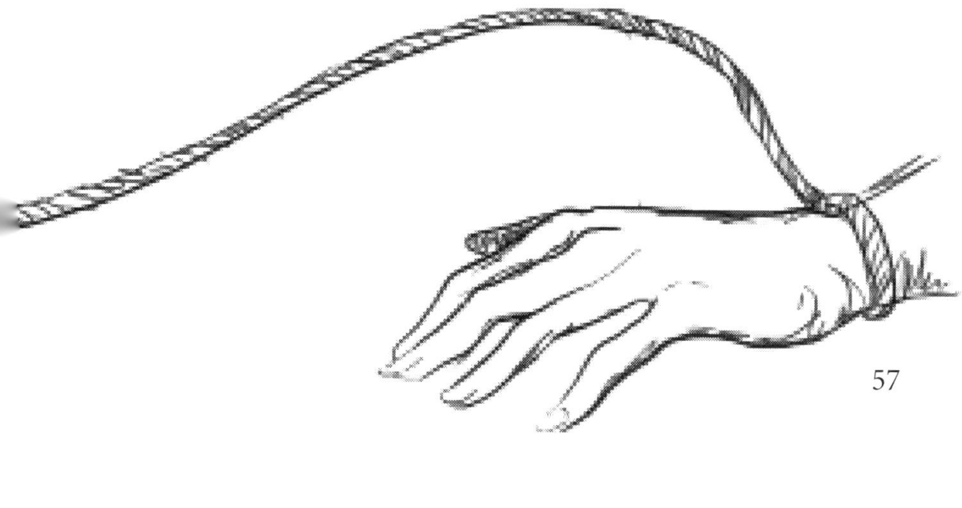

The Sound of Music.

It's both fortunate and unfortunate, the absorbency music has for memories.

There are a lot of songs that can transport me to car rides, picnics, and lakeshores.

There are a lot of songs that I can't listen to anymore.

Maybe it's just me. I process the sound of music visually. My mind draws in detail; outlined memories shaded in sensations, scribbled between rhyme and rhythm at the intersection of emotion beneath auditory wavelengths; those are a lot of senses to draw upon for a single illustration.

Sometimes, I have to sit in silence.

The sound of music fights for attention: the arguments.

R&B has nothing on a symphony of screams, swearing, insults; standard notation *forte and syncopation*— the sound of the people I love showing me how not to love is way too loud.

I grab my head and shake it sometimes just to shut them up.

If I walk through this house,

I'll find shattered glass, plates, and pins,
I'll avoid the insults and broken wedding rings,

I've seen the way people trip over things,
I've seen the pain of promises,

Of course, I've learnt to watch my step,
I've spent decades watching them,

But I don't think I'd ever walk through it,
Or build one like this,

Because if this is all that love is,
Then it seems like people are just trying to survive it.

Fall.

You remind me of fall.
You remind me of the fall.

Fall paints nature like gold. Every step you took painted the earth in a glow; illuminated by your bold and unbothered, I was walking next to you and saw the whole path of trees lean inwards.

They couldn't stop looking at you. Neither could I. So, I leaned closer and closer, crossed logs and tiny rivers, until I started to trip, to tumble—

I was among the scraped knees, and bone fractures.
You barely tilted, I hit the ground hard—

man, that was a bad fall.

I guess it just wasn't our season, it took me months to heal from it, though you still remind me of it—

I kind of hope we cycle back to it,
because I kind of want to fall all over again.

Artword.

one night, they wrote some words and called it artwork

like lighting at sunset,
a pretty girl in a sundress,
painting the light in her smile,
a head on chest 'till sunrise.

i read it over, said
you write a pretty artword.

they paused, asked how the exnd should look,
maybe 100 years go by and they're still together.

they laughed at that, like silly girl,
i wanted to ask, *well, what do you propose?*

but i didn't. i guess i didn't really want to know.

instead, i just closed my eyes,
saw the artwork come alive,

and hoped someday it really would.

you tend to break my heart like poetry
so i think my greedy fingers are the ones that keep me calling

cause if i'm being honest
i think they're painfully addicted to the way you inspire me.

I just can't get you out of my head. I want you to hold me, meet me halfway— I know mind matters over everything, but the problem is my mind thinks you matter when you're not mine and never have been.

Sharing Feelings.

I want you to feel the way I do.
The worst part is that you do.

Like skin on skin, eye to eye, nerves sparked, hands entwined;
it's chimeric imagery, lucid dreaming— I see exactly what
you're seeing. I feel exactly what you're feeling.

We're sharing feelings.
It's just that yours aren't for you and me.

We're on the same frequency, yet so disconnected, we're speak-
ing the same language, but you and I aren't speaking—

Will you just talk to me?

I can translate all your feelings, transcribe them like poetry, in
your words or mine, it's the same lovesick vocabulary, and every
time I write, I feel a chest kind of heavy—

I want you to feel exactly what I'm feeling. That want but can't have, not enough for somebody, heart stuck in my throat, I want to blame you for everything—

but every curse in your name blurs into a blessing. *Fuck you,* and *I wish you the best* end up overlapping, the pain and the love overlap in these feelings— I'm angry, but honestly, I want you to be happy.

I think it's because I still see you objectively. The stories you've told me, I know where your heart's been, so I see your compassion, and the kindness you've shown me—

but most of all, in you, I see a bit of me.

And I just want to be happy. So, I guess that means I want you to be happy.

Even if it is with her and not with me.
Even if the only thing we ever share are feelings.

Boombox.

i finally made it to your street,
boombox in the backseat,
you got in, said something,
i hid the boombox, perfect timing.

like bars on bars on bars on beats,
have you ever been written symphonies?
i had the orchestra on my sleeve,
until your smile told me something.

what about you? are you happy?
of course i am, what else could i be?
though i'm not enough for you,
this isn't enough for me,

even though my truths collect dust in the backseat.

you glanced behind me,
what's that jacket thrown over?
i said nothing important,
kept my eyes forward,

you paused for moment,
something stuck on your tongue,
then you just shrugged, smiled,
and put her record on.

sympathetic:

the way hearts beat, and palms sweat,
fight or flight, you've never been like this,

your sympathy's showing; a system switch,
it's like for them, you'd do anything,
but for you, they'd do nothing.

they rest and digest, sitting next to you,
cruel and misleading, they couldn't give two—
unfair, the way opposite feelings can fill the same room.

although, amazing is another term i would use:
the way we create people-based addictions, switch entire
nervous systems, and put ourselves in someone else's shoes.

so, while love is painful, and i'm sympathetic,
i think the rush of adrenaline, and the vasoconstriction,
the understanding, and the genuine compassion,

are some of the very best parts of being human.

I'm a Narcissist, but the humblest,

call Me upside down King Midas,
because everything I touch turns to gold,
and gold is how I weaponize it.

I touched you and you moved with radiance,
lit the room with reverence,
yet Me Me Me was all I could think.

like what if you left Me after this,
sharpened gold into a sword,
and cut My heart into bits—

and that is exactly what you did.

almost like I predicted it,
almost like I made you do it,
did I make you do this?

I'm a Narcissist, but the humblest,

looking at gold, all I see is My reflection,
a Narcissist's favourite weapon is self-destruction,
humbled by the way it creates monsters out of men.

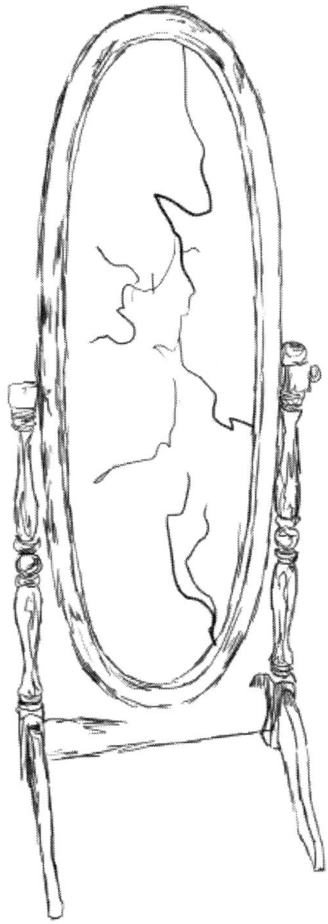

Honey Pockets.

if you could see my pockets,
you'd find them dripping in honey,
oh, but honey, don't you worry,
i have jars on jars saved up just for you.

so if you were with me,
you'd never go hungry,
cause honey's pretty heavy,
and tastes like loyalty, love, trust, and value.

so fool me once, shame on you,
fool me twice, i'd still feed you,
i'd turn honey into gold,
if that's what would fill you,

and then i'd turn my pockets inside out for you.

although, with all this honey saved for you,
i think the flowers would get upset,
the bees would be jealous too—
frankly, they'd be pretty mad at you.

but really honey, i'm not worried,
because honestly knowing you,
the bees and flowers would follow my lead,

and they'd probably forgive you too.

Gold is Your Colour.

I'm sorry you don't feel valued.
I'm sorry you feel like they don't see you.

Though it's kind of funny, isn't it?

That in thinking of all the possible ways they won't give you their time, thoughts, or things—

you give them yours.

You use all the paper and ink you can find, turning thoughts and things into time, as you write pages on why they won't even pick up a pen for you.

You list all the ways they don't matter anymore, in attempt to write them out of your hands for good— so why is their name on the pen you chose?

These are your things so why is their name on that pen?

Be honest, how many things, thoughts, and time have you really given them?

Thoughts, time, things. Thoughts, time, things. Thoughts, time, things. Thou—

Precious like gold.

That's what those are. Yet here you are, spending it all on a person who doesn't see colour; greying out your life, just to write them brighter.

I mean, I can understand why you do.
My fingers are stained blue too.

I guess you keep giving up all your gold because that's what your heart is made of.

The blessing is the curse, isn't it?
People will take all the gold they can get.

But, the truth is that people don't know what to do with that much gold. You can't even be mad at them— they don't understand what they've never learnt.

Meeting a person who radiates the shade of the sun, whose life has so much essence it warms everyone is a privilege.

Sometimes, privilege can be scary when you haven't learnt the value of it. Sometimes, sunlight is scary if you've only been surrounded by darkness. Sometimes, gold isn't the colour they seek, but that doesn't make it less precious.

Gold is still gold even if someone doesn't care to recognize it.

I wish I could tell you about the people who do recognize it.

They may not be authors, but they've written chapters, and novels, and fairy tales in which you are the hero, the villain, the best friend, the sidekick and—

I dipped my hands in ink for you.

That doesn't matter though. It doesn't matter because you haven't yet used any ink on yourself.

You haven't written down all the ways you're lovable, or bled the page with why you're enough, so how can you read anyone else's work?

I see that pen sitting in your hand, and that paper resting by your side. I see you reaching for the ink to write them a text, but I really hope it's to claim your own value.

How much time, thoughts, and things have I used up on you?

Another Letter.

Dear,

Sometimes, it feels like I'm writing a whole book for you. I wouldn't be surprised if subconsciously, that were true. I've always been someone who feels more than they should.

I think I've always had words in me, but I'm not sure. I can't be sure because when you arrived, I felt my creativity catch flame. It set the entire forest of my mind ablaze. I mean, maybe it was bound to be lit and you just happened to catalyze it. Or maybe, you happened to be there just as I learnt how to use matches.

You have always been creative. The courage of creativity isn't easy, but you've managed to embolden me with the rhymes you write, the songs you sing, and the way you dance off beat. Sometimes, when my flame starts burning out, I talk to the parts of me that your creativity helped me find.

It gets frustrating sometimes. You fuel so much of the fire, that I can't seem to burn out the thought of you. You have no idea how many tears I shed over you, yet here you are embedded into so many pieces, it's ridiculous.

Regardless, I will thank you. I will thank you because you have definitely been a muse. I will thank you because the art you filled my mind with unlocked another part of it. I will thank you because I don't think I'm writing a whole book for you, but I think you had a part to play in its existence.

Thank you.

Sincerely,
Me

Burgers and Fries.

Burgers and fries and windows rolled down on warm summer nights— those are the moments I feel most alive. The air hits different, the lights glow brighter, and I'm reaching in the bag for some fries and a burger.

I close my eyes, take a bite, and a portal of memory opens; a messy kind of crossover between real and almost moments—

suddenly, things turned out so different.

We grabbed some fries, picked up some burgers. Then, we parked under the sunset and sat there for hours. We sang off key, harmonized to our laughter, but this time, when we finished our food, the night wasn't over.

We drove to the ocean right after.

On the way there, you said we had to stop for something. So, you drove-thru, offered me fries dipped in ice cream. I said I'd never tried it— honestly, I was lying.

I just wanted to see you smile when you saw I loved something you gave me.

That one night turned into twice, three times, an anniversary, a lifetime— almost like this time you chose me, almost like this burger and fries could rewrite history.

I open my eyes. I'm brought back to this moment. I glance over at my best friend, she's laughing at something. She turns the radio up, starts dancing, we start laughing, we're singing.

I smile and let go of the what could have beens. I roll the window down, and feel the warm breeze hit me. I'm grateful for the almost, the real life, and the maybes. Where I am is where I need to be.

Right here, right now, this is everything I need.

Kaleidoscope.

How do you describe a meant to be?
I would describe it kaleidoscopically.

Turn it back, look through the lens slowly, and see it reflect the light of her next to me, brightening the colours of late nights and laughing, illuminating dark patterns of heartbreak, and crying.

Turn it inward, and see the challenges reflected in me, patterned like forgiveness, compassion, and honesty— see her mirrored in the lessons inside me.

Put the kaleidoscope down and see the reality. See where I'm standing, different than who I used to be, in a light of self-love, a higher energy, and you'll still see her standing right next to me.

That is how I would describe a meant to be.

When I was 3, I bought some candy,
3 days later I had 8 cavities,

When I was 18, I asked him to go out with me,
in 3 months, my heart started decaying,

At 33, maybe I'll have everything,
and maybe I won't have to ruin myself entirely.

Half & Half.

i think you emptied half of me,
and filled the other half of me,

i can't decide if those three months,
were a glass half full or empty,

because let's be honest here,
you did nothing for me,

just steeped me in sadness,
stirred up my self-esteem,

got me searching for what i was missing,
i started downing elixirs to fill me,

but turns out i'd been half & half already,
parts had spilled out long before you met me,

so maybe you didn't empty
or fill any halves of me,

maybe you just showed me where to add the milk and honey.

I'm so sorry you can't invest your whole self into anybody.

You split yourself into dollar bills and half pennies, spend half of you given all of me. I paid that price entirely, paid it all in worthless currency— swollen eyes and damp pillows are all it bought me, and then I went and spent it all on you.

I'm sorry you can't invest your whole self into anybody.
I'm sorrier I invested in you.

don’t your arms hurt
carrying all those hearts you stole?

perfection lies to you

tell me again how much i mean to you

give me a second to catch my breath
i've been outrunning you since we first met
stopped that one time, now look where i'm at
lovesick, tear stained, and out of my mindset

out of my mindset, and out of focus
had you, lost you, all within seconds
lost you, lost me, lost sight of the vision
now i'm outrunning you, to keep myself on track

I called you today.

you gave me the best news,
it filtered my spirit,
and binded my soul,

I put down my phone,
and picked up a pen, ecstatic,
headlined it
BREAKING NEWS

I'm finally over you.

The Final Scene.

Have you ever eaten waffles at sunrise? Waking up, there's so much sunlight— we own a radio now. I turned it on just as that song we both danced to that first time played. You can't dance, but you can absolutely sing. Piano fingers, caressing keys. I remember you cried because that's how much you loved me. Sunrise is where I knew you did— we weren't eating waffles then. It was just us under a pink-gold sky. All I needed was in the question you asked me.

I laughed the first time you walked in; your smile is magnetic— I wondered if I would ever laugh like that again. I did. Again, and again, and again. A walk from class, a birthday party, let's go to the beach, and grab some coffee. I never stopped laughing, and the minutes turned into hours into days into weeks—

And now here you are sitting right across from me. With maple syrup in your left hand, and a ring on mine, I'm looking at you—

We have this entire lifetime.

My eyes cleared after what felt like hours. Maybe days. Months probably.

I finally took notice of where I had stopped. I looked to my left and then to my right— fields of green stretched out on both sides. I tilted my head towards the sky.

The pink-yellow hues had been replaced by a sea of glitter. At intervals were clouds that seemed to hold the stars together, and as I gazed across the sky from left to right, I paused at the half crescent.

The moon was pearl coloured. It exuded power. It exuded brightness. But, alongside both these things, it exuded creation.

I had never seen a sky like this.
But, I didn't want to chase it.

Instead, I took out one of the napkins from the glovebox, and wrote an entire story beneath it. The napkins turned into paper, and the paper turned into blessings.

The setting sun was incredible, and while I recognize this—
I think I was meant for something far more magnificent.

My favourite thing about creativity,
is the way we can use it to alter our reality.

My Roots.

Do you see these roots inside me?

Like branches of ancestral wisdom, planted by knowledge
passed down generations—

Aren't there things you weren't taught, but know are true in the
core of your intuition?

I have centuries of lifetimes rooted in me like lessons.

ancestors self-risen from the depths of oppression,
women who freed themselves with a fiery resilience,
the courage of a brother who fought for independence,
the creativity of sons who turned poverty into privilege.

I have centuries of pain woven into my genetics.

like abuse at the hands of an in-law or husband,
robbed after the two jobs you just finished,
starving because you chose education, immigration,
all the minds that twisted fear into obsession.

I'm still digging to find what I can't see. I'm desperate to uncover the parts stolen from me; roots severed, poisoned, erased like history—

I'm just looking to reclaim the uprooted parts of me.

What a beautiful picture you've painted of me!

I truly appreciate the way you've coloured me in golden skin, so creative the exotic sexuality you've portrayed me in.

Even more so I admire the way you've created humour out of my ancient medicine— honestly, it amazes me how you invade my country, then rewrite my whole identity, all within a single painting, play, and story created without understanding a single word in my language or a decade in my century. You even threw your racial prejudice into the mix!

What a lovely representation of me you've interpreted!

Hold on—you're telling me you forgot to include the parts of the story where you rape the women and indoctrinate the children? Oh, that's my fault, I must have misunderstood when you said you were retelling my history.

Next time, I'll make sure not to expect human decency.

Punishment.

punishment is a colour scheme,
guns and gas for the brown and black,
peace and please for your royal whiteness,

a solid scheme highlighting brutal reality,
you still claim transparency,
but forget that colour circles have none of that,

how can they?

circles are cyclical like '12 meets '21,
colour will stain foundations once it's painted on,
especially if it's painted in dark brown blood,

same cycles, same systems,
different schemes to implement them,

will someone tell me who's in charge?

transparently, it's not the democracy,
seems like #FFFFFF based tones,
get the weightiest votes,

and the creative freedom,
doors opened for them,
did you offer them a seat yet—

as they point guns at congress.

The Game of Life.

list the ways a human life can be taken,
a knife, a gun, a cell, a paper,

man-made decisions in a man-made creation,
like man is God, but more like Gamemaster,

playing around with human existence,
in arcades of tribunals and witness stands,

i solemnly swear to play fair and square,
speak the truth and nothing but the truth,

so God help me—

Gamemaster will help me,

reveal my hand and tell my truth,
but then again, the truth can be created too,

if you offer enough, i'll change my truth for you,
and watch lives get tagged out of this game of life,

placed in cages, or maybe coffins,
if that's what the law decides,

if those are the rules the Gamemaster created,
the ones that God never validated,

yet take human life like it's divine decision,

the Gamemaster doesn't even need to play it,
he just picks the pawns with strategized privilege,

pits them against each other and watches in time,
as we play his game and take each other's lives.

Giving Season.

with an arm stretched out, and windows down,
she offered him coins, granting grace like God—

she stopped playing God months ago, almost like blessings
dissolve with the snow—

almost like giving's just seasonal,

like giving's an anti-vice antidote,
a golden ticket to heaven afterward,

cause confessions and coins drip like water,
until your conscious needs cleansing no longer—

tell me, how many sins are you trying to make up for?
don't get me wrong, you are me, i am her;

guilty, i'm guilty, i'm sorry, forgive me,

get off the road, and go make some money,
work harder in a world that gives you nothing,

guilty, not guilty, i'm learning, forgiving,

i bless you with love, i hope you keep going,
work kinder in a world that taught me to give nothing,

there is no guilt, there is no reward.
there is only giving and it's not seasonal.

(For)giveness.

they consider me a fool for *forgiveness*,
they consider me a fool for *give-ness,*

as if the people sitting under the apple trees
don't deserve it,

they never earned it

you say as you pick fresh fruit with your ladder,
reaching with ease, you grab every last apple,
catching, and stretching so none hit the ground.

because life is so precious, and everyone's human,
until *they never earned it* comes on around,
and then you only whistle to that song—

do you even know who built you that ladder?
it was a gift to your father from the fathers
of the apple-tree sitters,

like their *give-ness* and *forgiveness* somehow made
you richer but *give-ness* and *forgiveness* somehow
makes me foolish—

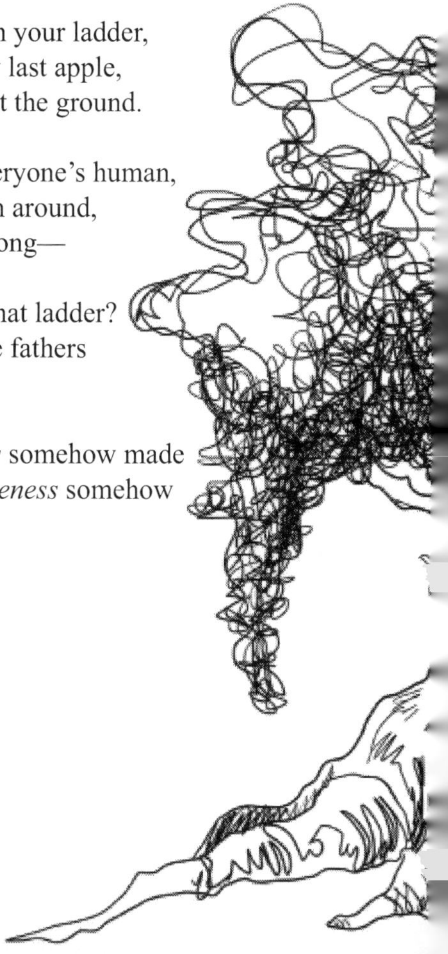

the truth is you never did earn it,
those apples, those trees, you don't deserve it,

the truth is you stole it.

from the tips of the branch to the roots of the seed,
so the apple-tree sitters can never plant their own trees,
so they can never feed their hunger generationally,

so they stay tree-sitting,
climbing on their knees,
digging for you, and earning next to nothing,

and then you'll call me foolish
for *forgiveness* and for *giving*—

and that is how you keep half a country starving.

we tend to forget
we're not all dealt the same deck

and in another life the cards might be stacked against you.

but you'll eat off our plates.

power will make you hungry,
abuse of power will make you hungrier.

but at the end of the day,

bruised and beaten bodies,
broken backs and torn shoes,
will still bend down to offer you food,

not out of respect, not out of remorse,
but out of empathy and compassion,
for human life at its core,

so where's yours?

they may not be your people by definition,
but we're all made of the same elements,
nervous, muscular, and circulatory systems—

the feeling of pain is universal,
divides are created by human imagination,
so you should know exactly what you're inflicting.

but if you believe so strongly in an *us versus them,*
why do you eat the food grown by the blood that you spill?
use remedies made from the knowledge you've tried to kill?

notice how you stand above them to beat them down,
yet willingly bend to the ground every time you need to eat;

hunger will bring anyone to their knees—
one more reason why power means nothing.

and at the end of the day,
you will cradle sticks covered in the blood,
and canons flooding the lungs of these men, women, children,

and you will still eat off our plates.

ask me what painful looks like.

perhaps it looks like you and me,
because painfully you keep asking me,
what painful looks like—

like a gun to my head, you drop dead,
but i've been dropping dead since partitioning.

since they partitioned my feet and left,
more than half of mine for you,
less than half of mine for me.

of course i'd be angry—
30 years they'd been stepping on me,
and then they proposed i could only step on the east,
though there was less of you and more of me—

they realized quite quickly, quite painfully,
this is tricky, so they backed out, quite easily,

but i've been dropping dead since the 40's,
of course, painfully, only painfully—

what a *Catastrophe.*

a painful feeling, that looks like you and me,
you detaining me, you displacing me,
and you bleeding the human rights out of me—

they might have cut my feet,
but you're *killing me.*

so ask me what painful looks like,
just tell me what painful looks like,
because you my friend, you are me.

a gun to my head, and you see yourself dying,
your own blood on the streets,
because you funded a weapon and created an enemy,

for both you and me.

so, painfully, realistically,
painful is you and me, our deaths, our injuries—

but let's revisit what painful looks like entirely:

so it's them against you, and them using me,
you against me, with your laws, power, and weaponry,
the west against me, your global tag team—

i'm fighting painful all on one foot,
you're standing on painful with international security.

painfully, you keep standing on me,
stealing from me, silencing me,
and i've been dropping dead since you invaded my territory.

painfully, so painfully,
do you feel the pain you're causing me?

if painful keeps looking this way,
if painful keeps looking like you and me,

soon, there'll be nothing left of me.

Bandages.

piles upon piles of bandages piled up
in the left corner of my bathtub
there's just too much trauma
and not enough material
in the whole world to soak it all up

piles upon piles of bandages piled up
it seems each time i bandage my cuts
time or water just washes them off
and i have to replace them every time they fall
though i wonder why i need this many at all

the piles of bandages have been piling up for months
perhaps avoidance is what keeps them piling up
my fingers keep bleeding
my fingers aren't healing
i don't have a problem if i just cover it up

of course all these bandages are going to pile up
and eventually they'll fall in and clog my bathtub
then i'll have to clear them
i'll have to deal with them

what will this country do once all their bandages are used up?

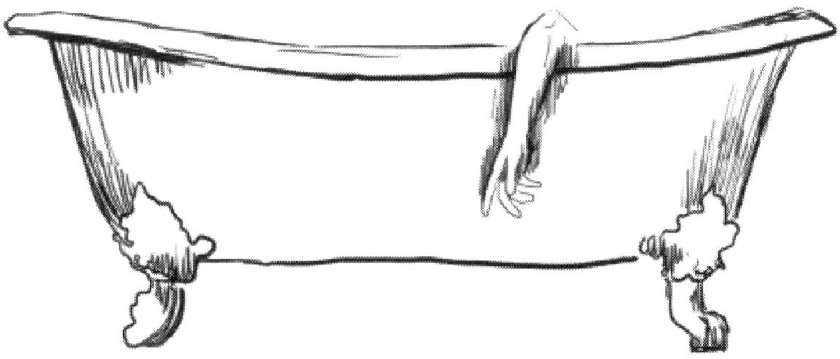

God gave humans hands but what can they really do?

I have opposable thumbs, but I can't hold onto all the people I love. I have strong hands, but I can't carry all the suffering in this world. My fingers have grip, but human nature is so greedy that they can never grab enough. My palms illustrate prophecies, but I still can't predict the future.

God gave me these hands, but nothing is in them.

Maybe that's the blessing.

one night,
one night,

stories poured from my sisters' eyes,
pooled in puddles knee-high,

in the shape of boyfriends and family ties,
the body's water doesn't lie,

about rough hands that grab and grind,
nights when grandfathers become attackers,
childhood friends that take advantage,

you walk down the wrong paths

there are no right paths left,
covered bodies and thinking twice mean nothing to them.

my sisters and i sat in a circle that night,
laid down our life jackets and pocket-knives,

our ambitions breaking, our feet are aching,
our achilles heel is society,

carrying all of this fear is exhausting—

one night,
one night,

my sisters' stories poured from my eyes,
tears that felt as real as mine,

and after all was said and told,
my sisters and i mopped the ocean-like floor,

we don't let the water trickle outwards,
because we've seen you defend your brothers first,
gaslighting flames in a patronizing tone,

water lies so cry me a river

though something you'd do well to remember,
is that water will always douse out the fire,

and from these stories our truth will pour.

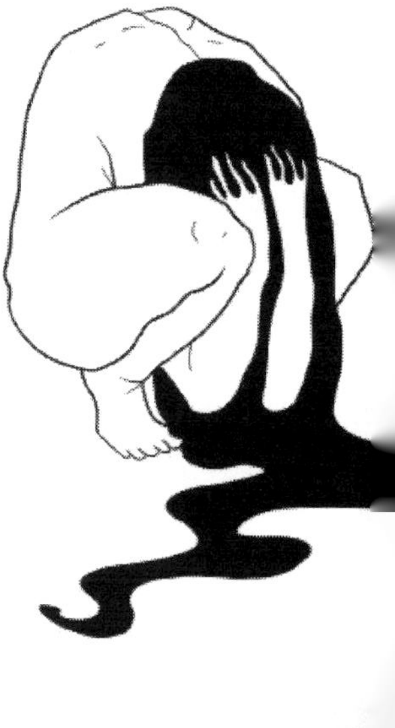

Show Girl.

Show girl,
Show off girl,
Stand beside that Ferrari girl,
That's all you can do girl,

Show girl,
Show it all girl,
For what were girls made for,
If not passive entry doors,

But no girl,
Don't use those features girl,
The ones we ride for,
To buy a Mustang of your own,

Show girl,
She's beautiful,
Drives my pleasure,
I ride her whenever,

Show girl,
Show me girl,
Red clothes like red doors,
chipped nails like chipped rims,

Don't get blood on my backseat,
Stop moving,

Shut up bitch

Show girl,
I'd ride her,
That's my girl,
Let's share her—

Which her?

The Feminine Energy.

i think since the beginning of time,

the power of women demanded eminence,
screamed with resonance, a power evidenced by existence
itself—

but not just in a biological sense.

i'm talking about the feminine energy,
the energy of healing, of intuition, of sensuality—

of creation.

that's the power of life giving, as in giving life to change, to
solutions, to artistry, building something out of the sacredness of
nothing,

and i think that's a beautiful thing.
i think that's the energy through which this earth was created.

so tell me, when did things change?

when did femininity become submissive tendencies,
oversensitivity, rights that are barely yours to claim, the
beautiful, ethereal energy of creation re-painted in the red of
forced blood stains; a gift traumatized by violence—

when was the feminine energy made to feel powerless?

My Mind's Creation.

If I'm going to create things from the crevices of my mind, they're going to be mine.

They're not going to be yours.

The creation isn't pouring down your sweat, your feet aren't swollen from it, exhausted with a heart working double the speed—

The creation is flowing out of me.

For weeks and weeks, it's just it, my body, my being, and me, and it expands outward using my heart strings, developing off the trauma in my memories, growing up on the warmth in my gut, resting in my mind between my soul and blood—in my blood, in my soul.

Not yours.

So, if it's not living off your lifeforce, tied to your being, resting inside you, using your energy,

then I'm not entirely sure you can tell me what to do.

and for all the things I cannot control,
a creative culture is what I promote.

the rhythm has to come from the beat of your heart—
that is how you create living, breathing art.

I've never really been a dancer,
but my creativity dances like she's too clever for me to catch her.

I'm slightly clever, so yes, there are times I do catch her. But eventually she'll get away, my frustration sparking her laughter.

I would love to be creative whenever it's convenient, but my creativity just doesn't want to listen.

Occasionally, I'll try to lure her in— prisons baited with sad songs and traps filled with vivid movies. But then I remember that she's too clever, and only dances to her own feet. Her feet often sound like feelings— at least they do to me.

When she comes in waltzing, or tapping, or breakdancing, the sound's familiar to me. It sounds like anger, pain, love, or memories.

That's the only way she'll stay, the way she chooses to inspire me.

I can sit here all night, searching for prompts to write poetry, but it's her word-stained feet that leave marks on my page remarkably.

Now mind you, the dancing can get overwhelming.

Sometimes, she'll want to be caught, but the noise of ideas is just too much for me. It's too unsynchronized and off pitch— sometimes I swat her away.

That's especially true when it sounds like sadness.

She comes in allegro, a one-two step, dragging in all the monsters from the back of my closet— I don't always want to write out my hurt, anxieties, and losses.

It's paralyzing. I don't understand why this is the inspiration that gets my creativity dancing.

But sometimes the sound is so good that even I start dancing.
The sound of self-worth is like my 16th birthday party:

A room with hearty music, with chocolate and candy,
surrounded by laughter and love packaged in human beings,
they gift me time and energy.

That's a feeling that gets me moving.
That's something I don't do too often.

I don't really dance. I tried it when I was six and it wasn't expressive enough for me. Still, I did it for a decade because that's who I was supposed to be. Guilty.

Guilt is another feeling that gets creativity flowing. Forget having to catch, she loves the rhythm of guilt so much that she'll run right into me. She co-wrote empathy. That piece took a while, because again, it was overwhelming.

Creativity can be tricky, a balancing act between expression and not losing your life in too much expression— when you're constantly swimming in your own thoughts, it's easy to start drowning, it's easy to forget the difference between truth and stories.

Sometimes, creativity embarrasses me.
I'm uncomfortable sharing this piece.

I see things too drastically, I have too many feelings, creativity looks so different in me— I didn't show anyone any of my content until last week.

For a long time, I tried to control creativity, force her to fit in, but eventually I learnt it's okay to not control things.

Because while creativity is a part of me, she is also her own entity. She takes pride in the essence of her being. That is the lesson to me.

This is the lesson: I don't know if I'm a good dancer, and I don't know if people will like my dancing, but I'm trying this new thing where I close my eyes and sway to my own rhythm.

Creativity is clever, and I could probably catch her, but I'm starting to learn that the best part about her is her freedom.

Eating dinner is simple.

I've always wondered why people put in so much time and effort into doing something so simple; setting the table, arranging utensils—

until I realized that living is like a plate.

Plate: The one I carry to the table, intricately designed, filled with fruits and vegetables.

Plate: That which I'm standing on, unpredictable, movement shifting the ground.

Do you understand how plates are made? Personally, I do not.

But I do know that in between planning this, and wanting that, you were too busy texting under the table, and looking for someone else—

you didn't realize you missed the sunrise, that bad joke your brother made, the curry, ice cream, late night drives— do you remember what anything tastes like?

I used to wonder why people put in so much time and effort into something so simple, until I realized:

It doesn't matter where you sit, or how you set the table, but if you can't remember the taste of what you ate, are you really living?

Eating dinner is simple.

November 15, 2020

so, I have a problem.
I can't stop speaking in rhythm.

I thought it would be fine,
after writing out a couple lines,

but even in my head,
all I do is rhyme out

thoughts.

I sent a text that Mr. Graham would have bought.

I can't complain though,
he's a record-breaking artist so
maybe I can just—

no.

my brain has scientific equations to solve,
so I need to stop speaking in code,
I need to start speaking in real life big words,

like astronomical and non sequitur,

so I can elucidate what I mean to say
without people thinking I'm not perspicacious—

it's gets difficult when you open your heart through words,
when nonchalance intersects with humour,

no one looks at you with respect—
I'm trying to stand here with my diagram and present.

my words may not make sense to you,
but my words have value.

maybe I can't describe the translating sequences without thinking about translating lyrical score,

but that doesn't mean I couldn't do it if you gave me a test tomorrow—

so what I am a bit all over the place,
it's 2am,

the moon is sinking,
and I can't stop thinking,

about how this rhyming shit signed a permanent lease with me.

you know what, i'm not even worried about why this occurred,
cause the biology of humans is difficult to discern,

there's so much unexplained it's no wonder science students barely learn—

poetic variation.

I used to really hate spoken word,
but I think my genetics are variat-ing,

making poetry a part of my DNA—
and here points to evolution.

I think my research is over,
I solved the question proposed:

I am evolution-ing.

that's why I have this flow,
and that's it I have no more.

The Ocean.

The only reason I'm not writing for the Ocean yet,
Is because I haven't learnt to not slip up on verses yet,
My lips move slower than my mind can,
The rhythms twist faster than my tongue man,
I'm brilliant,
Don't mistake that,
I just gotta learn how to sing an E flat,
before the Ocean and I can get in contact.

Now imagine if I felt peace.

Oh, the places I'd go.

A trip down unbothered lane, hands swinging, feet skipping, I'd take a minute to converse with the earth. I'd play with the lions, and fly with the birds, jump off trees, find that I don't fall—

I soar.

I'd walk through life playing with sand in my palms, splashing ocean water with my toes, and I would contain all the joy and love in this world; I'm grateful for the clouds, the moon, the sun—

and out of that gratitude I would build fields of creation.

I would dance with sunflowers, paint the grass vibrant colours, share stories with all the insects and bugs. I'd learn with them, catch, and release them, and then I would release myself from barriers of self-doubt.

I would follow my loves and fall in love. I'd build a house by the beach and take a walk with my person.

I am fulfilled by the purpose that fuels my passion.

Filling my mornings with pancakes and laughter and my evenings with dancing in kitchens and lattes.

Without judgement, without fear, I'd sing, create music, change perceptions with my lyrics, and then I would help others break their own boxes, my zone is limitless because I don't run from my talent anymore.

I would simply breathe without feeling my breath latch onto panic, or obsession and then,

if I felt peace, oh I'd do all over again.

the process of peace is a relationship: the internal with the external; everything i create in my bones has a way of expanding outwards, and if that be peace, then peace trickles out into the shape of suns and ocean breeze, until everything i sip and everything i soak somehow becomes everything i need.

If I never go to sleep, do I get to live forever?

Days aren't guaranteed. I might not wake up tomorrow.

Some say that leaving in sleep is leaving in peace. I don't agree.

Wouldn't you want to know your date of departure?

We book tickets in advance all the time. There are no airports that surprise you with flights.

When you walk into Terminal A, you pass Check-in and Baggage Claim and you have the year, month, day, hour, minute of your takeoff.

At least then you can hug your mother, stay at your friend's house the night before, and confess all your feelings. At least then you know exactly what you're leaving.

But that's not the reality of life. With that in mind, I wonder why we all wake up each morning like waking up isn't opportunity. Time is just a piece of art, and success is a construct, so why are we limited by our own beliefs? I'm trying to produce more metaphors but quite frankly, all I can say is that life is there, and then it's gone and I'm so sorry for the pain caused by eyes that closed and never opened again. Do we take things for granted?

What do you want to do before you fall asleep tonight?

OUTRO

I'm not sure how to really conclude this, because I honestly think it's just the beginning. I found a box from my childhood a few months ago. I opened it, and what I found inside was writing— picture books I had created when I was 6, notebooks of lyrics noted down the summer of 7th grade, and pages on pages of scribbled and scratched poems and stories. I forgot these existed. I forgot the sheer amount of these that existed. As I shuffled through the wrinkled, worn pages scattered across my bedroom floor, I recalled the other pieces to this puzzle: the 11 year old who created a writing account on Instagram but never told anyone about it; the 13 year old who published a blog but would never sign her real name on it; the 15 year old who wanted to join the school's spoken word club but had her feet rooted in judgement, and the 16 year old who shrugged off the words she had inside her like fear and embarrassment— as if it's possible to ever shrug off your skin. We're not snakes. Even so, snakes only shed their skin to regrow into a better version of themselves. The same but bigger. That reminded me of the 17-year-old, who nearly lost this part of her altogether. I am grateful. I think the universe always guides with intention. Just as it seemed like this part of me was gone forever, somehow, it expanded. At 17, I was re-exposed to the world of writing and creation through a social justice non-profit I co-founded called Stay Woke. At 18, I was persuaded to present a speech for a contest, and within that year, I performed at multiple open mic events. I was keeping this part of me near, yet at arm's reach— dabbling in parts of self-expression, but never allowing creation to flow from all of me. And then, at 19, I transformed entirely.

And somehow, in between the heartbreak and love, both real and in my head, intertwined with the healing, fear facing, I wrote something. And this time it came from the core of my being. I felt like I was 6 again, writing from all of me— I was the same but bigger, because this time on shaking knees, I stood tall, holding this part of me in my palm, my name on it, my heart on my sleeve, I started to live in alignment with my heart, mind, and being, the art of creation guiding me—

and that is exactly what you're reading.

SIDE 2

New edition works.

there's something to be said about feeling pain and anger so deeply that you could write sonnets from your own skin bleeding—

and choosing the language of healing instead.

love is the one thing that never fails to inspire songs and sonnets and i think it's funny because no language or words have ever acccurately described it.

Love Remains.

I genuinely believe that even when there is nothing else there is still love. Between every failure and loss and doubt there will always be pieces of love to turn to. The grass will always grow green at the turn of the season. The sun will warm your skin even when it's cold. The waves of the ocean will always play with you.

There will always be a person rooting for you, making sure you're fed and showered and safe— even if that person happens to be you. Sometimes, it has to be you first. So yeah, in between all the pain and challenge and grief written into the folds of our world, I genuinely believe love will always remain unmoved.

there are days when the air feels sickly sweet like the world is falling in love with itself. it's like the earth has your feet and the air has your lungs and you are a single piece of matter tucked into the folds of time and space and dust and nothing else matters.

Earth to Hand.

I love summer because it feels like the earth is in my hands. My heart is the centre. Telling stories of great lovers; like man, like flower, like grass fed to table— my palm is the point where air meets land. Where it meets water. Where impossible meets possible and the whole entire universe is reworked— it feels like a garden.

My mother is gardening again. She's pulling weeds she never knew she had, and I lie next to her after years of anger; my past is a fear filled element that feels like winter— so I leave it at the door because I can. Because in summer, my choices are not frozen. The days last longer, my skin gets warmer, and time is no longer of the essence. It just is. And I can just do with the earth as I can.

Bianca Modi

Written by Bianca Modi
@biancaajm
https://biancamodi.com

Illustrated by Amani Mohamed
@amani_arts_

Author's Note

I couldn't tell you the exact day or time I started writing a book. All I can remember is being 6 years old, writing my first story. I kept it for myself. I wrote another, and another, and then I was 10, filling shoeboxes with pages of poetry. I was 13, sharing my work anonymously. Finally it was sometime later, and for a long time, I stopped writing.

There has always been a lot of fear inside of me— a lot of me holding myself back. It was a complex combination of wondering how people would perceive me, the fear of vulnerability, embarrassment— the list is irrelevant. The bottom line is that I was creating my own resistance, and I think in some ways, this mechanism expanded beyond just my writing.

At some point within the past 2 years, that resistance like fear was overcome. Perhaps, it was overlooked. It took me a while, but at some point, I saw fear standing in front of me and made the conscious decision to walk around it. I think I can pinpoint the first time I really did that— July 2020.

I guess that's why this is more than just a book to me. It's a moment of walking around walls I've been building. I am beyond grateful for the opportunity to do so.

I also have so so many people to thank— people who read drafts and drafts of the same piece, those who held my hand every time I broke down crying (or hysterically laughing), those who inspired the writing, and ultimately, those who gave me the space to just be me.

Thank you.

Manufactured by Amazon.ca
Bolton, ON

41477357R00083